THE GULF OF MEXICO

A TRUE BOOK

by
David Petersen

Children's Press®
A Division of Scholastic Inc.

New York Toronto London Auckland Sydney
Mexico City New Delhi Hong Kong
Danbury, Connecticut

**Baby sea turtles
scrambling into the
Gulf of Mexico**

Reading Consultant
Nanci R. Vargus, Ed.D.
*Primary Multiage Teacher
Decatur Township Schools,
Indianapolis, IN*

*The photograph on the cover
shows the Gulf of Mexico at
Talum, Mexico. The photo-
graph on the title page shows
an underwater view of the
Gulf of Mexico near the
Florida Keys.*

**Visit Children's Press® on the
Internet at:
http://publishing.grolier.com**

Library of Congress Cataloging-in-Publication Data

Petersen, David, 1946–
   The Gulf of Mexico / by David Petersen.
      p.   cm. — (A True book)
   Includes bibliographical references and index.
   ISBN 0-516-21665-1   0-516-27317-5 (pbk.)
   1. Oceanography—Mexico, Gulf of—Juvenile literature. 2. Mexico,
Gulf of—Juvenile literature. [1. Mexico, Gulf of. 2. Oceanography.]
I. Title. II. Series.

GC521.P47 2001
551.46'34—dc21   00-030665

GROLIER
PUBLISHING

Contents

Paradise, Pirates, and Ports   5

Oceans, Seas, and Gulfs   13

The Gulf Stream   17

Under All That Water   21

Storm Warning!   24

The Living Gulf   29

Pollution and Progress   38

To Find Out More   44

Important Words   46

Index   47

Meet the Author   48

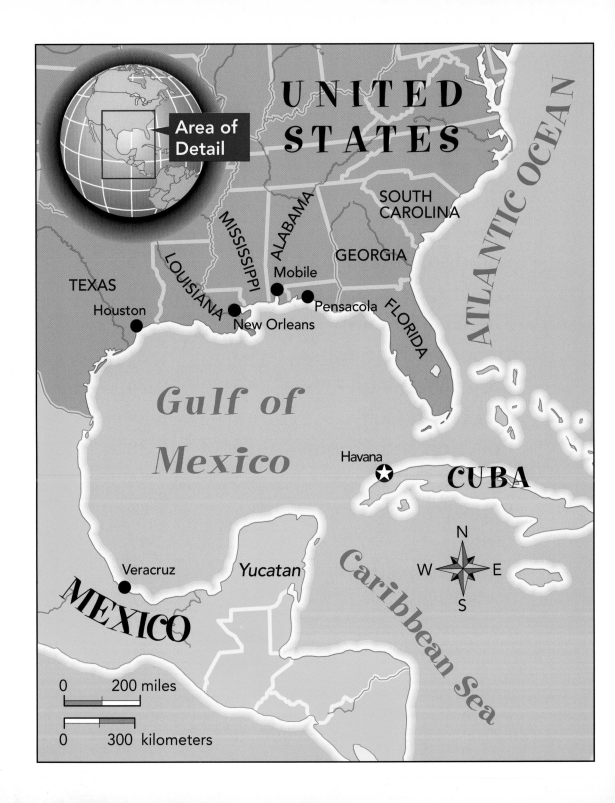

Paradise, Pirates, and Ports

The giant body of saltwater called the Gulf of Mexico forms the eastern shore of Mexico. It stretches from the Yucatan Peninsula all the way to the Mexican border with Texas.

Yet the Gulf of Mexico is as much American as it is Mexican.

The Gulf Coast in Mexico (top) and in the southern United States (bottom)

Its beaches, swamps, and marshes also border the southern United States from Texas to Florida.

Until a few hundred years ago, the only people living on the Gulf Coast were American Indians. Except for the heat, storms, and bugs of summer, they lived in a beautiful paradise.

Along endless ribbons of beach they collected clams and other tasty shellfish. In

American Indians, such as the Seminole (above), were the first people to live along the Gulf Coast.

marshes and tide pools, they found oysters, crabs, and turtles. The Indians also fished, hunted, and gathered plants.

In 1492, explorer Christopher Columbus landed on the island of Cuba, becoming the first European to see the Gulf of Mexico. Soon, more invaders

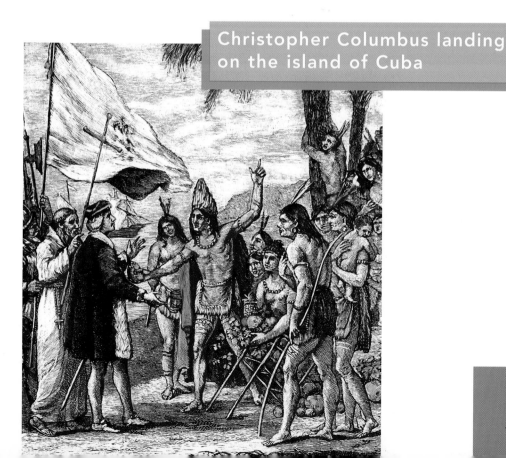

Christopher Columbus landing on the island of Cuba

came sailing into the Gulf from Spain, France, and England.

Some of these new Americans became pirates—sea bandits

Jean Lafitte was a famous pirate who raided ships along the Gulf of Mexico.

who stole from ships loaded with gold and other treasures. And until the mid-1800s, slave ships sailed into Gulf seaports. They carried kidnapped Africans who were being brought to America to work on southern plantations.

The pirates and slave traders are long gone. But ships and travelers from all over the world still use Gulf Coast ports. Important Gulf seaport cities include Houston, Texas;

New Orleans (above) and Havana (left) are important Gulf ports.

New Orleans, Louisiana; Mobile, Alabama; Pensacola, Florida; Veracruz, Mexico; and Havana, Cuba.

Oceans, Seas, and Gulfs

Oceans, seas, and gulfs all are salty—and huge. Together, they cover more than 70 percent of Earth's surface. So, how do they differ from each other?

Oceans are Earth's largest and deepest bodies of water. The world's four great oceans are the Atlantic, Pacific, Indian, and Arctic.

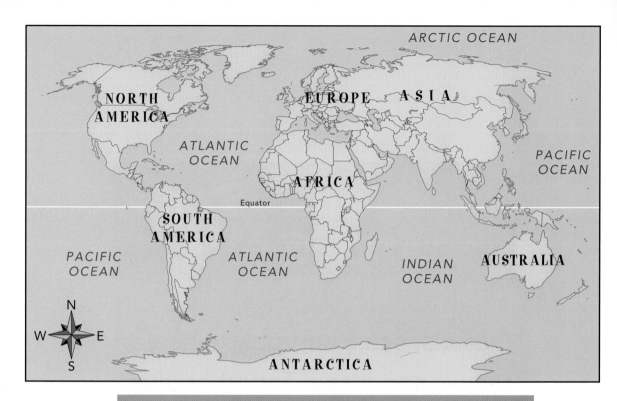

Seas are smaller "arms" of oceans that border land. For example, the Caribbean Sea, between Central America and Cuba, is an arm of the Atlantic

Ocean. Gulfs are usually smaller than seas and always jut into the mainland, forming giant inlets.

A "gulf" is a big gap—in this case, a gap filled with seawater.

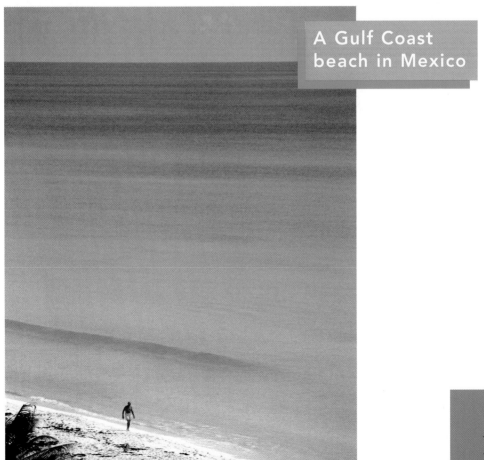

A Gulf Coast beach in Mexico

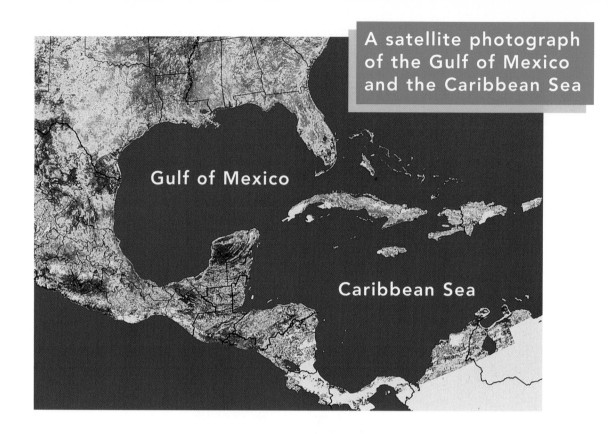

A satellite photograph of the Gulf of Mexico and the Caribbean Sea

Gulf of Mexico

Caribbean Sea

A gulf can be the arm of an ocean or an arm of a sea. The Gulf of Mexico—with the Caribbean Sea on its south and the Atlantic Ocean on the north—belongs to both.

The Gulf Stream

Ocean currents are "rivers" of warmer, colder, or saltier water that run through oceans. Through the quiet, dark water of the Gulf flows a current of warmer, clearer water called the Gulf Stream. This major ocean current forms in the Caribbean Sea

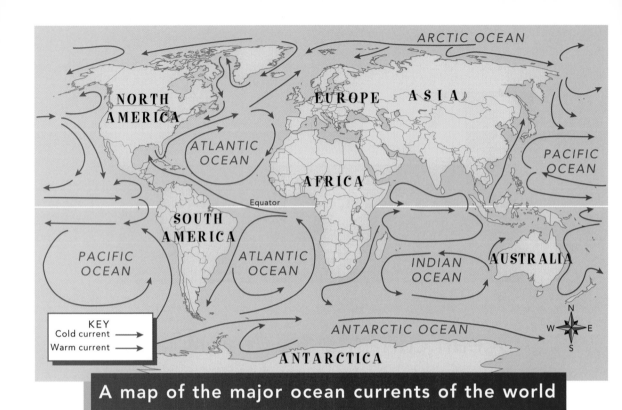

A map of the major ocean currents of the world

and enters the Gulf through the Yucatan Channel.

After looping north through the Gulf of Mexico, the Gulf Stream joins the Atlantic Ocean in the Straits of Florida. It flows

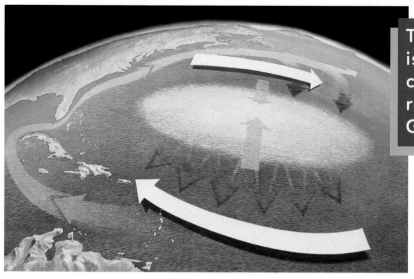

The Gulf Stream is a warm ocean current that runs through the Gulf of Mexico.

northward along the east coast of North America, then west across the Atlantic.

Because the water is so clear, sunlight is able to reach deep into the Gulf Stream. Plankton, a floating mass of tiny plants and animals, is nourished by that sunlight. Small fish and

Sunlight is able to reach deep into the clear waters of the Gulf Stream.

other sea creatures eat the plankton. Bigger fish eat the smaller ones, completing the aquatic food chain.

Under All That Water

The floor of the Gulf of Mexico is bowl-shaped—shallowest nearest shore, and deepest in the middle. The continental shelf, as its name hints, is an underwater "shelf." It is 8 to 135 miles (13 to 217 kilometers) wide and begins at the shoreline.

In this overhead view of Florida and the Gulf the light-blue area next to the shoreline is the continental shelf. The darker blue area is the continental slope.

Sloping gently downward, the shelf reaches a maximum depth of 600 feet (183 meters). Where the continental shelf ends, the continental slope

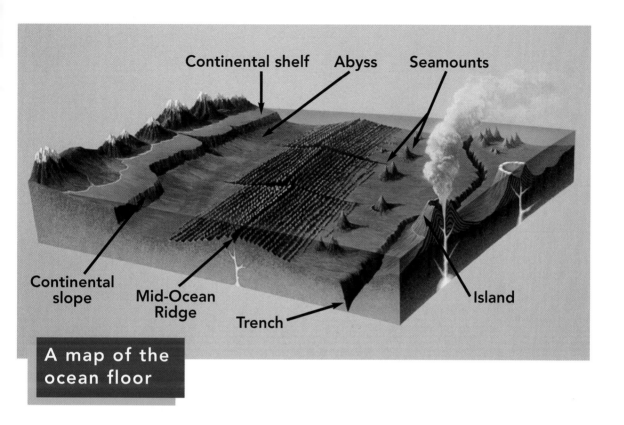

Continental shelf   Abyss   Seamounts

Continental slope

Mid-Ocean Ridge

Trench

Island

A map of the ocean floor

begins, dropping steeply to the Gulf floor. The deepest part of the Gulf of Mexico is a depression called the Sigsbee Deep. It plunges 14,358 ft. (4,376 m) below sea level.

Storm Warning!

Gulf Coast residents know they can expect severe summer storms. Thunderstorms hit the area often, and hurricanes are the terror of the Gulf region.

Hurricanes begin as swirling windstorms far out over the ocean. When wind speeds within this cyclone reach

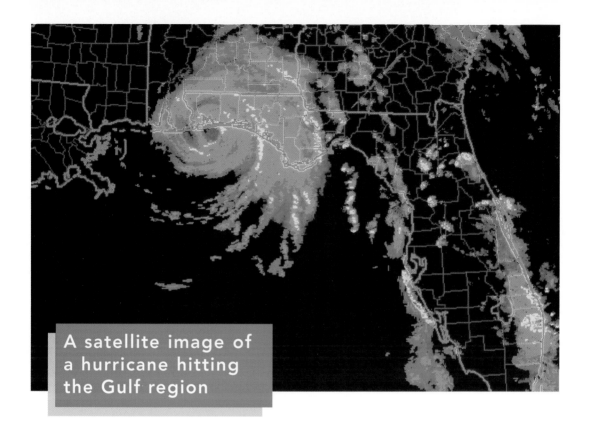

A satellite image of a hurricane hitting the Gulf region

74 mi. (119 km) per hour, a hurricane is born. You can think of a hurricane as a giant tornado, many miles across and packed with lightning, thunder, and rain.

Over the centuries, hundreds of ships and boats have been lost in hurricanes along the Gulf Coast. And when a hurricane touches land—watch out! Hurricane winds, sometimes stronger than 100 mi. (161 km)

Waves in the Gulf of Mexico during a hurricane

per hour, rip the roofs off houses and send everything flying.

Hurricane waves are even more destructive, smashing and drowning everything in their path. Hurricanes are given names

Hurricane Andrew caused tremendous damage along the Gulf Coast in 1992.

to avoid confusion and to help weather experts pass along information more quickly. Recent Gulf hurricanes have included Andrew, Hugo, Donna, and Camille.

The Living Gulf

The shoreline and floor of the Gulf are always changing. Sediments are soil particles dissolved in water. Rivers wash sediments into the Gulf. The sediments settle to the bottom and slowly build up triangle-shaped wedges of new land called deltas.

The Mississippi River has created a huge delta in the Gulf of Mexico.

Deltas form in estuaries— places where freshwater from rivers mixes with saltwater from the ocean. Estuaries are shallow and often overgrown with trees called mangroves. These mangrove swamps swarm with life—storks and

Gulf Coast mangrove swamps in the Florida Everglades (left) are the home of alligators (top) and ibises (bottom).

many other birds, fish, snakes, alligators, and American crocodiles.

A barrier island
in Louisiana

But even as rivers are building deltas, waves and sea currents are pulling sand from beaches in one place, only to drop it somewhere else. Sometimes sand collects offshore in giant piles, creating barrier islands. And barriers they truly are, helping to protect the coast from the strong winds and thundering waves of the Atlantic Ocean.

Some barrier islands—like Galveston in Texas and Pensacola in Florida—are several miles long and support big cities.

Galveston, Texas, is a huge barrier island.

On both islands and mainland, the Gulf's beaches are scattered with lovely seashells. All those fancy "cabins" were once the home of meaty creatures called mollusks. Among the most common are oysters, clams, and scallops.

On beaches, in tide pools, and along the shallow continental shelf live crabs, lobsters, and shrimp. These are crustaceans—animals that wear their skeletons on the outside, like suits of armor.

Lobsters (above) are among the shellfish that live along the Gulf's continental shelf. Many Gulf beaches are scattered with seashells (right).

The deeper waters of the Gulf Stream are home to millions of fish, ranging in size from tiny to tremendous.

Dolphins, manatees, and many kinds of fish swim in Gulf waters.

Dolphins and whales also swim in Gulf waters. And closer to shore, in quiet inlets, cruises the gentle giant manatee. Dolphins, whales, and manatees are air-breathing mammals, not fish.

Everglades National Park

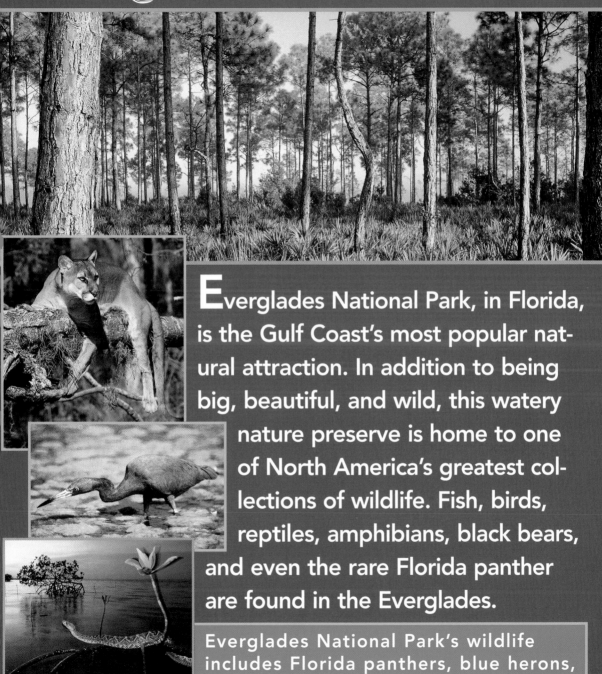

Everglades National Park, in Florida, is the Gulf Coast's most popular natural attraction. In addition to being big, beautiful, and wild, this watery nature preserve is home to one of North America's greatest collections of wildlife. Fish, birds, reptiles, amphibians, black bears, and even the rare Florida panther are found in the Everglades.

Everglades National Park's wildlife includes Florida panthers, blue herons, and diamondback rattlesnakes.

Pollution and Progress

Fishing, shipping, and oil are the Gulf of Mexico's most important industries. Of the thousands of ships visiting Gulf seaports each year, many are supertankers. These giant transport ships carry millions of gallons of crude oil pumped from beneath the Gulf.

An oiltanker (left) and oil-production platform (above) in the Gulf of Mexico

Crude oil is refined into gasoline, motor oil, and the other petroleum products that power our cars, boats, airplanes, and cities. The drilling, refining, and shipping of petroleum products provides jobs for thousands of Gulf Coast residents.

Citrus fruits, rice, and sugar-cane are among the products grown along the Gulf Coast. And because the Gulf of Mexico is such an exciting place to visit, tourism is big business.

But all this human activity damages the environment. Too many fishing boats catch too many fish, endangering some species. Oil refineries foul the

air with bad-smelling black smoke. Offshore oil wells and supertankers may spill tons of crude oil into Gulf waters, killing fish, birds, and aquatic mammals and polluting Gulf beaches with tar.

Gulf Coast cities—bustling with people, cars, and factories—are another source of air and water pollution. Farm chemicals—fertilizers, insect poisons, and weed-killers—seep into rivers and are washed into the Gulf.

The hopeful news is that Gulf Coast governments, businesses, and citizens are working to control pollution and repair the harm it has already done. With such help, the Gulf

Waves breaking on a Bermuda beach

of Mexico may once again be the clean, healthy paradise the American Indians knew and loved. And that would truly be progress.

To Find Out More

Here are some additional resources to help you learn more about the Gulf of Mexico:

 **Books**

Dipper, Frances. **Mysteries of the Ocean Deep.** Aladdin Books, 1996.

Johnson, Jinny. **Simon and Schuster's Children's Guide to Sea Creatures.** Simon and Schuster, 1998.

Morgan, Nina. **The Caribbean and the Gulf of Mexico.** Raintree Steck-Vaughn, 1997.

Van Cleave, Janice. **Oceans for Every Kid.** John Wiley & Sons, Inc., 1996.

Organizations and Online Sites

Gulf of Mexico Program

*http://pelican.gmpo.gov/
edresources/kids.html*

A site explaining how people can help protect the Gulf of Mexico.

Life without Light

*http://www.bio.psu.edu/
cold_seeps/index.html*

Take a virtual tour through the cold-seep habitats of the Gulf of Mexico.

Looking for the Gulf Stream

*http://marine.rutgers.edu/
pt/activities/lfgs.htm*

Information and activities about the Gulf Stream.

Texas State Aquarium

2710 North Shoreline
Corpus Christi, TX 78402
*http://www.texasstate
aquarium.org/seaus/
seaus.html*

The Texas State Aquarium provides programs about the aquatic animals and habitats of the Gulf of Mexico. Its website features a virtual tour of Gulf habitats.

Important Words

aquatic having to do with water

cyclone whirling windstorm

depression hollow, hole

endangering putting in danger

nourished fed

orbit to circle around a central point

peninsula long, narrow strip of land jutting
into a body of water

petroleum raw oil that is the source of
gasoline and fuel oils

plantation planted area taken care of by
laborers

ports places where ships load or unload
cargo or passengers

resource source or supply

swamp wet spongy land often partly cov-
ered with water

Index

(**Boldface** page numbers indicate illustrations.)

alligators, 31, **31**
American Indians, 7, 8, **8,** 13
Atlantic Ocean, 13, 14, 16, 18, 19, 33
barrier islands, 32, **32,** 33
birds, 31, 37, 41
Caribbean Sea, 14, 16, **16,** 17
Columbus, Christopher, 9, **9**
continental shelf, 21, 22, **22,** 34
continental slope, 22, **22**
Cuba, 9, **9,** 12, **12**
deltas, 29, 30, 32
dolphins, 36, **36**
Everglades, **31**
Everglades National Park, 37, **37**
fish, 31, **36,** 37, 41
Florida panther, 37, **37**
Galveston, Texas, 33, **33**
Gulf Coast, **6,** 26, 37
Gulf Stream, 17, 18, 19, **19, 20,** 35

Havana, Cuba, 12, **12**
Houston, Texas, 11
hurricanes, 24, 25, **25,** 26, **26,** 27, **27,** 28, **28**
Lafitte, Jean, **10**
lobsters, **35**
manatees, 36, **36**
mangrove swamps, 30, **31**
marshes, 7
Mexico, **cover, 6,** 12, **15**
Mississippi River, **30**
Mobile, Alabama, 12
New Orleans, Louisiana, 12, **12**
ocean currents, 17, **18, 19,** 32
ocean floor, 21, 23, **23,** 29
oil spills, 41, **41**
Pacific Ocean, 13
Pensacola, Florida, 12, 33
pollution, 41, 42
sea turtles, **2**
Seminole, **8**
Sigsbee Deep, 23
Straits of Florida, 18
thunderstorms, 24
Veracruz, Mexico, 12
Yucatan Channel, 18
Yucatan Peninsula, 5

Meet the Author

David Petersen took his first swim in the Gulf of Mexico at Corpus Christi, Texas, when he was eight years old. He has since explored the Gulf Coast from Padre Island, Texas, to Pensacola, Florida.

David has written many books for Children's Press, on subjects ranging from continents to parks to people. One of the most interesting people he knows is his wife, Caroline. Together, they live happily ever after in a cabin on a mountain in Colorado.